SEARCH
FOR STEAM
Industrial Railways 1964–1966

CHARLIE VERRALL

First published 2019

Amberley Publishing
The Hill, Stroud
Gloucestershire, GL5 4EP

www.amberley-books.com

British Library Cataloguing in Publication Data.
A catalogue record for this book is available from the British Library.

ISBN 978 1 4456 8539 7 (print)
ISBN 978 1 4456 8540 3 (ebook)

Typeset in 10pt on 13pt Sabon.
Typesetting by Aura Technology and Software Services, India.
Printed in the UK.

Contents

Introduction

The Industrial Revolution in the eighteenth century resulted in an increase in the demand for more and more coal, and various methods were developed to satisfy this demand – the use of rivers and canals, and later waggon-ways with wooden tracks, the wagons being hauled mainly by horses. Later the wooden tracks were replaced by 'L'-shaped edge rails, and then bull-headed rails similar to those in use today. In many places boilers were utilised to provide the power to drive not only the machinery in factories, pit headgear etc., but also winches for the inclined planes used to climb intermediary hills to avoid earthworks.

AB2073, works plate, Dailuaine Distillery. 17 April 1965.

The logical step was to develop steam-powered locomotives to haul wagons, and in 1812 the first, not particularly reliable, steam locomotives began to be introduced on the Middleton Railway and other colliery systems in the North East of England, thus preceding the use of such means of haulage on the Stockton & Darlington and Liverpool & Manchester railways by several years. The success of these early locomotives was to result in their usage in not only collieries but also steel works, quarries, docks, in fact anywhere where the movement of goods or materials was needed outside of the expanding mainly passenger-carrying railways. As loads became heavier and heavier several of the colliery railways, which in many cases had 'main lines' of their own, began to use locomotives fitted with tenders, some built for them, others purchased from mainline companies. In fact, the use of tender locomotives continued well into the 1950s. The majority of the locomotives used in industry were built by a variety of manufacturers, although many surplus ex-mainline locos were also purchased. These came from a variety sources, including the North Eastern Railway and the Glasgow & South Western Railway. Very popular were those from the South Wales Railways which had been absorbed into the GWR. Fortunately several survived to be purchased for preservation. Even in the dying moments of steam on British Railways, several locomotives went into industrial use.

To provide for the demand for locomotives, a number of manufacturing firms became established, supplying locomotives to mainline companies as well as industrial users and overseas customers. Throughout this book individual locomotives are indentified by an abbreviated makers name and their builders or works number. The following manufactures are mentioned in the text:

AB	Andrew Barclay & Sons & Co. Ltd, Kilmarnock
AE	Avonside Engine Co. Ltd, Bristol
AP	Aveling & Porter Ltd, Rochester
AW	Sir A. G. Armstrong, Whitworth & Co. Ltd, Scotswood, Newcastle
BH	Black, Hawthorn & Co. Ltd, Gateshead
BP	Beyer, Peacock & Co. Ltd, Gorton, Manchester
Cdf	Cardiff Works, Taff Vale Railway
CF	Chapman & Furneaux Ltd, Gateshead. Successor to BH
EB	E. Borrows & Son, St Helens
EV	Ebbw Vale Steel, Iron & Coal Co Ltd, Ebbw Vale
FW	Fox, Walker & Co. Ltd, Bristol
GR	Grant, Richie & Co., Kilmarnock
HC	Hudswell, Clarke & Co., Leeds
HE	Hunslet Engine Co. Ltd, Leeds
HL	R. & W. Hawthorn, Leslie & Co. Ltd, Newcastle-upon-Tyne
JF	John Fowler & Co. Ltd, Leeds
K	Kitson & Co. Ltd, Leeds
KS	Kerr, Stuart & Co. Ltd, Stoke-on-Trent
Lewin	Stephen Lewin, Poole
LEW	Lambton Engine Works, Philadelphia, Co. Durham
Mkm	Markham & Co., Chesterfield
MR	Motor Rail Ltd, Simplex Works, Bedford

MW	Manning Wardle & Co. Ltd, Leeds
N	Neilson & Co. Springburn Works, Glasgow
NR	Neilson, Reid Ltd. Successor to N
NBL	North British Locomotive Co. Ltd, Glasgow
OK	Orenstein & Koppel, AG, Berlin & Nordhausen, Germany
P	Peckett & Sons Ltd, Bristol. Successors to FW
RH	Ruston & Hornsby Ltd, Lincoln
RR	Rolls-Royce Ltd, Shrewsbury. Successors to S
RS	Robert Stephenson & Co. Ltd, Newcastle-upon-Tyne and Darlington
RSH	Robert Stephenson & Hawthorn Ltd, Darlington and Newcastle-upon-Tyne. Amalgamation in 1937 of RS and the locomotive business of HL
RWH	R. & W. Hawthorn Ltd, Newcastle-upon-Tyne. Predecessor to HL
S	Sentinel (Shrewsbury) Ltd, Shrewsbury
Sdn	Swindon Works, Great Western Railway
Stoke	Stoke Works, North Staffordshire Railway
VF	Vulcan Foundry Ltd, Newton-le-Willows
WB	W. G. Bagnall Ltd, Stafford
YE	Yorkshire Engine Co. Ltd, Sheffield
9E	London & South Western Railway, Nine Elms Works

Other abbreviations used are:

APCM	Associated Portland Cement Manufacturers Ltd
BICC	British Insulated Callenders' Cables Ltd
BOCM	British Oil & Cake Mills Ltd
BPCC	British Portland Cement Manufacturers Ltd
BSC	British Steel Corporation
CT	Crane Tank
DE	Diesel Electric
DH	Diesel Hydraulic
DM	Diesel Mechanical
F	Fireless
GEC	General Electric Co. Ltd
Ghd	Gateshead Works, North Eastern Railway
GWR	Great Western Railway
HIW	Holwell Iron Works
ILS	Industrial Locomotive Society
IRS	Industrial Railway Society
LCGB	The Locomotive Club of Great Britain
NCB	National Coal Board
NCBOE	National Coal Board Opencast Executive
PT	pannier tank
RPCC	Rugby Portland Cement Co.
RTB	Richard, Thomas & Baldwin
SDSI	South Durham Steel & Iron Co. Ltd
S&L	Stewarts & Lloyds

ST   saddle tank
T   side tank
TVR   Taff Vale Railway
USC   United Steel Companies
VBT   vertical boilered tank
WT   well tank
4wDM   four wheel Diesel Mechanical

This book is a photographic record of some of the mainly steam locomotives seen between 1964 and 1967. Included is information relating to others seen at the same time and other sites visited. Sadly, other than details of individual photographs, all my notes and records were lost several years ago; however, I have been able to create an idea what was seen using various Industrial Railways handbooks published by the Industrial Railway Society. Any errors in the various lists, etc. are solely mine. Some details are also taken from an incomplete list of scrapped locos which was drawn up in the early 1970s.

Chapter One

A Passing Interest, Prior to 1964

Although I had collected engine numbers in the late 1940s, I had shown little interest in industrial locomotives. Perhaps this was in part due to my not having detailed knowledge of where they could be found; in addition, I was not an active member of any clubs or societies. I was most certainly aware of their existence having seen one or the other of the little Beyer, Peacock engines at Hilsea Gasworks when passing by train on family visits to the Isle of Wight. Other remembered sightings included looking out the train window down on the siding of British Industrial Sand at Holmethorpe from a train on the Redhill

S6833, Hall & Co. Coulsdon Quarry. 30 August 1953.

JF17726, Hall & Co. Coulsdon Quarry *12*. 30 August 1953.

avoiding (Quarry) line. Of particular interest were a pair of locos, by S; one was a vertical boiler rebuild of a MW saddle tank and was named *Gervase,* the other was equally interesting being the locomotive portion of a railcar from the Jersey Eastern Railway.

It was when travelling on one of these services that I noticed a little derelict engine shed to the east of the southern portal of Quarry Tunnel at Merstham. In August 1955 I worked for the Southern Region of British Railways in an office at Redhill and one lunch time went with a colleague to see part of the route of the Surrey Iron Railway, and I enquired regarding the history of the derelict building. He told me this was part of Merstham Lime Quarry, which had closed in 1949, with the locomotives being the two S's at Holmthorpe. It was suggested that I might like to arrange to visit the chalk quarry of Hall & Co. at Coulsdon, so on 30 August I made my first, and for several years only, visit to an industrial site. They had arranged for their two locomotives to be out in the open. These were the dismantled S6833 and the working loco JF17726. Another similar JF loco, JF22597, was a regular sight for many years trundling back and forth in Hall & Co.'s sidings adjacent to East Croydon station.

I did not really start taking railway photographs until September 1961 and, despite having a number of lineside permits, industrial locations passed me by. One of the permits was for the mainline between Finsbury Park and Hitchin, although I saw them, no photographs were taken of JF20337 at the Shredded Wheat Factory at Welwyn Garden City, or HC1593 *London John* that worked at John Mowlem's Marshmoor yard. I am sure these were just two of several missed opportunities.

Chapter Two

1964 – Some New Photographic Opportunities

At the start of 1964 I was working in the Southern Region's offices at Essex House, Croydon, where one of my colleagues was Malcolm Burton, the LCGB Chairman. One day he suggested I might like to join a small group visit to some industrial sites in north Kent, to which I agreed. I suspect there was an ulterior motive to this suggestion since most sites were only accessible by road and I held a driving licence. On 21 March, after collecting our hire car in Croydon the previous day, we went to Northfleet Deep Water Wharf where 0-4-0STs P1950 *Bradley* and P2080 *Northfleet* were photographed. At APCM Holborough Cement Works 0-4-0STs RSH7813 *Tumulus* and P1740 *Stone* were seen together with 2-2-0WT AP9449. AP9449 was later in the month moved for preservation at the Bluebell Railway.

P2080, *Northfleet*, and P1950, *Bradley*, Northfleet, Deep Water. 21 March 1964.

RSH7813, APCM, Holborough Chalk Quarry, *Tumulus*, 21 March 1964.

AP9449, *Blue Circle*, Sheffield Park, August 1965.

Visits were also made to APCM Bevan's Works where 0-4-0STs P829 and P967 were resident; APCM Kent Works, Stone to see 0-6-0ST MW1601 *3 Arthur*, 0-4-0STs RSH7336 *8*, and P1965; finally APCM Highstead. An interesting introduction to some of the smaller industrial sites.

However, on 24 April I was in Northumberland visiting NCB Isabella Colliery to see the lone resident loco 0-4-0ST HL2571 *C5*, seeming to emerge from the back gardens of the local houses. The colliery yard was connected to both the British Railways Newsham to Blyth branch and the nearby Bates Colliery, and 0-6-0ST RSH7887 *C17* was seen with a service either from or to Bates Colliery.

HL2571, NCB, Isabella *C5*. 24 April 1964.

RSH7887, NCB, Isabella *C17*, waiting to depart to Bates Colliery, 24 April 1964.

We were to visit Bates Colliery and saw resident locos 0-6-0STs RSH7951, RSH7741 and VF5303, the latter being an ex-WD Austerity loco similar to British Railways J94 Class. Other NCB sites visited included Bedlington 'A', Bedlington 'F', Choppington and Seghill.

The following day, 25 April, we had crossed the River Tyne and were at NCB Philadelphia, the main sheds of the Lambton, Hetton and Joicey railways. Nearby was Lambton Engine Works (LEW), which undertook major repairs and modifications – a feature of LEW was the fitting of lowered cab roofs because of low clearances at some of the collieries. Most of the engines at Philadelphia on that day could not be photographed since they were under cover, in any case the weather was downcast. This was a shame since there were a number of 0-6-2 tanks there, and of course No. 27 – an engine of real interest. No. 27 was built in 1846 as a 2-4-0 tender loco by RS for the Newcastle & Darlington, their No. 22 – absorbed as No. 30 by the North Eastern Railway in 1854 and rebuilt as an 0-6-0 tender loco at Gateshead in 1864, and then as a 0-6-0ST in 1873 – was sold to the Lambton Railway in 1898, and rebuilt at LEW as a 0-6-0T in 1904. How much of the original locomotive remained is questionable. I was to see No. 27 on this and a later visit to Philadelphia but regrettably did not manage to get a photograph. Several of the 0-6-2Ts had, over the years, originated from the Taff Vale Railway, including CDF306 67 *Gordon*, ex-Longmoor in 1947 and preserved in 1962 as TVR *28*; CDF302 *53* ex-TVR *26* and GWR *448*, scrapped in October 1966; and CDF311 ex-TVR *64* and GWR *475*, scrapped in 1958. Seen at Philadelphia were 0-4-0STs HL2530 *28* with a standard cab and RSH7756 *38* with a Lambton cab. Also seen was 0-6-0ST RSH7688 *4*. We must have visited some other sites for which I do not have a positive record.

HL2530, NCB, Philadelphia, *28*, 25 April 1964.

RSH7756, NCB, Philadelphia, 38. 25 April 1964.

RSH7688, NCB, Philadelphia, 4. 25 April 1964.

One of the places frequently visited by enthusiasts was Bowater's Pulp and Paper Mills at Sittingbourne. This was a 2 foot 6 in line running firstly over a viaduct from near to Sittingbourne railway station, then past Kemsley Mill to Ridham Dock where there were standard gauge sidings connecting to the Sittingbourne to Sheerness line. Passenger services were run on the narrow gauge lines for employees who lived in Sittingbourne and worked at Kemsley or Ridham. On the narrow gauge there was a fleet of thirteen steam locomotives; four 0-4-2STs built by KS, six 0-6-2Ts, one by MW, one by KS, and four by WB, two fireless locos by WB, and a 0-4-4-0T by WB. There were two standard gauge locos, a 0-4-0ST by WB and an ex-SECR P class loco, ex-BR No. 31178. The company accepted organised groups of visitors each year and ran special two coach trains, hauled by one of the 0-6-2 tanks from Sittingbourne to the shed at Kemsley and Ridham Dock – there was also an engine shed at Sittingbourne. On 19 June I was on one of the visits organised by LCGB, seeing all of the steam locomotives and taking photographs of most of them. Two of the narrow gauge engines were of particular interest: 0-6-2T MW1877 *Chevallier,* formerly on the Chattenden and Upnor Railway, and 0-4-4-0T WB3024 *Monarch.* WB3024 was not overly successful at Bowaters and in June 1966 went to the Welshpool & Llanfair Railway.

MW1877, Bowaters
Sittingbourne,
Chevallier.
19 June 1964.

WB3024, Bowaters
Sittingbourne, *Monarch.*
19 June 1964.

On July 11 I was on another group visit, organised by IRS, to WD Bicester and then to APCM Shipton-on-Cherwell. We were met at Bicester station from where we were taken by railcar to Arncott Workshops, which, other than Longmoor, was responsible for all home-based Army locomotives. There were a large number of 'Austerity' 0-6-0STs present, including HE3802 *WD202*. Also present was RH218046 *WD814* and a 2 foot gauge Hunslet-Hudson 4wDM HE1939 *MSER8*. Sadly, because of my lost records it is not possible to identify what else was seen.

HE3802, WD, Bicester, *WD20*, 11 July 1964.

HE1939, WD,
Bicester, *MSER8*,
11 July 1964.

RH 218046, WD, Bicester, *WD814*, 11 July 1964.

After returning to Bicester station we continued on to APCM Shipton-on-Cherwell where two 0-4-0STs, WB2178 2, RSH7742 6 *C.F.S.*, and four 0-6-0STs, AB2041 3, P1378 5 *Westminster* and HE1649 4 were based.

P1378, APCM, Shipton-on-Cherwell, *Westminster*. 11 July 1964.

RSH7752, APCM,
Shipton-on Cherwell, C. F. S.,
11 July 1964.

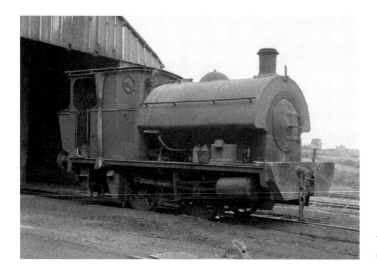

WB2178, APCM, Shipton-on-
Cherwell, 2, 11 July 1964.

After work on 17 July we set off on a weekend tour of the ironstone quarries of the Midlands. The first visit was to Oxfordshire Ironstone near Banbury. This was an extensive system with sheds at Wroxton and Penhill Farm. By the time we got there, save for one engine, all of the locos were in the sheds and it was not possible to get any photographs. In total some twenty-four steam locos were seen, two 0-6-0Ts by HC, six 0-6-0STs by HE, 3 0-6-0STs by P, seven 0-4-0STs by HC, three 0-4-0STs by P, a single 0-4-0ST by HE, a single 0-4-0ST by AE and a 4wVBT by S. Sadly, small diesels shunters from S and later RR had started to arrive in 1961 and by 1965 the steam locos were redundant and scrapped almost overnight, that is except for the very first loco to arrive, 0-6-0T HC1334 No. 1 *Sir Thomas*, which was retained for preservation, later going to Quainton Road. The next visit was to Thos. E. Gray & Co., Burton Latimer, where three 4vVBTs were seen, S6515 No. 2 *Isebrook*, S9369 *Musketeer* and S9365 *Belvedere*; all three were later to go into preservation. S6515 was originally to be GWR 12, however the order was cancelled before delivery, and had been withdrawn from service in 1958 and stored half in and half out of its shed.

S6515, Thos. E. Gray, Burton Latimer, *Isebrook,* 17 July 1964.

S9365, Thos. E. Gray,
Burton Latimer, *Belvedere,*
17 July 1964.

    The final visit on that day was to Byfield Ironstone where their three locos were present including 0-6-0ST MW 1210 *Sir Berkeley,* also later to go in to preservation.

    The visits to the various sites started in earnest the following day, with fifteen or more sites being visited, albeit briefly in most cases. For the majority, the locos were not in a position to be photographed since they were in their sheds, etc. At SDSI Irchester the renowned line of derelicts was still in place, some just frames, others without tanks, and others with boilers and no tanks. Amongst them were 0-6-0ST P1402 *Progress* and 0-4-0STs P1258 *Rothwell* and AB2326 No. 9.

P1402, SDSI, Irchester,
Progress, 18 July 1964.

P1258, SDSI, Irchester,
Rothwell, 18 July 1964.

AB2326, SDSI,
Irchester, 9.
18 July 1964.

It seemed to be a feature of many places we visited that that they had locos that had been abandoned. One example was 0-6-0ST HC899 *Sheepbridge No. 22* at S&L Minerals, Desborough, although the even older 0-6-0T HC431 continued to be used until the quarry closed in 1966. RTB Irthingborough Quarries were about to close and 0-4-0ST AB1466 had little longer to survive, being broken up in August. Two locos that were to be preserved were 0-6-0Ts HE1953 *Jacks Green* and HE1982 *Ring Haw* at Nassington Ironstone Quarries.

In 1951 production started at a new quarry at BSC Exton Park near Cottesmore, which, in the main, had a fleet of 0-6-0STs built by YE. We were to see most of these, including YE2434 *1362*, YE2502 *1360* and YE2512 *1356*; shortly after our visit diesel locos started to arrive and these three were the first to be scrapped.

HC899, S&L,
Minerals,
Desborough,
*Sheepbridge
No. 22*,
18 July 1964.

AB1466, RTB,
Irthingborough, 8,
18 July 1964.

HE1953, Nassington
Ironstone Quarry,
Jacks Green,
18 July 1964.

HE1982, Nassington
Ironstone Quarry,
Ring Haw,
18 July 1964.

YE2502, USC,
Exton Park, *1360*,
18 July 1964.

An interesting site was that at Cransley Ironworks; these had closed in 1957 and the buildings were demolished in 1959. However two 0-4-0ST locos remained in their shed, in fact by 1964 they were literally holding it up. They were CF1194 and P832, both of which went to Cohen's when they took over the site in 1962; Cohen's were to break up a number of locomotives at Cransley, both industrial and mainline, including those from the line of derelicts at Irchester.

The largest quarry system was at S&L Minerals, Corby, supplying ore direct to the adjacent steelworks. There was a large fleet of 0-6-0STs, the first two being MWs coming from the Elan Valley Reservoir construction; later engines were enlarged versions built to the same basic design by MW, K and RSH; finally there were nine much larger engines from RSH; the large shed was at Gretton Brook, which we visited, and workshops at Pen Green. We were not to photograph any of the quarry locos on this trip but went to the interchange sidings with the steelworks where a dirty yellow 0-6-0ST HE3375 *40* was seen. Strangely, this particular loco was present each time we were to make a visit there. Finally at Corby, Shanks & McEwan were slag contractors for the steelworks and their 0-4-0ST HE1677 *Ian D. McLean* was dumped in a siding. We also went to H.I.W., Ashfordby near Melton Mowbray, here we saw four 0-4-0STs P1050 *Ironstone*, AB1899 *Stanton No. 26*, AB2042 *Stanton No. 36* and HC1321 *No. 16*.

HE3375, S&L
Corby Steelworks,
40, 18 July 1964.

HE1677, Shanks &
McEwan Corby
Steelworks, *Ian P. McLean*,
18 July 1964.

P1050, H.I.W., *Ironstone*,
18 July 1964.

AB1899, H.I.W., *Stanton
No. 26*, 18 July 1964.

The final day, 19 July, saw visits to S&L Lamport Quarry, where four 0-6-0STs were present, RTB Blisworth, where amongst the locos present was 0-4-0ST HL3721 *Ettrick* on blocks without wheels, and S&L Harlaxton, where 0-6-0ST AB2351 *Rutland* was waiting attention. Away from the ironstone quarries we went to EMGB Northampton, where, stored in the retort house, was the preserved Chaplin 0-4-0VBT. At CEGB Northampton three 0-4-0STs were present, including WB2565. Our final visit on the way south was to RPCC Tottenhoe where there were five 4wVBTs by S, including S9556 *No. 9 Craven,* and 0-4-0ST AE1875 No. 2.

HL3721, RTB, Blisworth, *Ettrick*. 19 July 1964.

AB2351, S&L Minerals, Harlaxton, *Rutland*. 19 July 1964.

WB2565, CEGB,
Northampton,
19 July 1964.

AE1875, RPCC,
Tottenhoe, *No. 2*,
19 July 1964.

S9556 RPCC,
Tottenhoe, *No. 9*
Craven. 19 July 1964.

On 15 August we were on a group visit to sites in the Erith area of Kent. The first visit was to BICC Erith Works where the two 3 foot 6 in gauge oil-fired 0-4-0STs WB2133 *3/3 Woto* and WB2135 *3/2 Sirtom* were positioned for photographs to be taken. In the nearby BOCM works 4wWT AP8800 *Sir Vincent* was seen. Finally at GEC Fraser & Chalmers Engineering Works 0-4-0ST WB2469 *V75* was present.

WB2135, BICC, Erith, *No. 3/2 Sirtom*. 15 August 1964.

AP8800, BOCM, Erith
Sir Vincent. 15 August 1964.

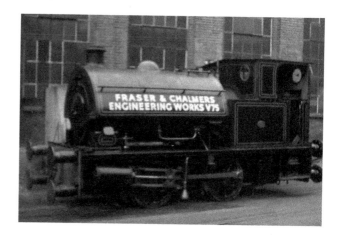

WB2469, GEC, Erith, *V 75*.
15 August 1964.

In 1936 and 1937 Manchester Collieries purchased five of the six NSR 'L' class 0-6-2Ts, three of which were at Walkden Yard when I visited on 20 September. One was painted as *NSR 2*, although in fact it was the boiler from the original NSR 2 mated to the frames of *Sir Robert*, NSR 72. The others were *King George VI* (NSR 69) and the withdrawn *Kenneth* (NSR 22). Amongst others seen at Walkden were the withdrawn 0-4-0STs HE1557 *Jessie* and KS3123 *Kearsley*. On 22 September I went to Gin Pit Colliery where the withdrawn 0-8-0T NW1419 *Emanuel Clegg* was waiting to be broken up after being sold for scrap two years earlier. On the way back I walked along the colliery tracks, possibly near Astley Green, and found the Giesl ejector fitted 0-6-0ST HE3302 *Stanley*, on which I cadged a ride towards civilisation.

On 25 September we started a three-day visit to Durham and Northumberland. It is worthy of note here that the sequence of visits stated for a particular day were not necessarily those which happened in real time. At NCB Seaham 0-4-0ST GR769 *43* was in a compound.

Stoke/1921, NCB, Walkden, *Kenneth*. 20 September 1964.

HE1557, NCB, Walkden, *Jessie*. 20 September 1964.

NW1419, NCB, Gin
Pit, *Emanuel Clegg.*
22 September 1964.

HE3302, NCB,
Walkden area, *Stanley.*
22 September 1964.

GR769, NCB Seaham,
43. 25 September 1964.

The Seaham Harbour Dock Company had been established in 1899 and had lines to a number of local collieries, which were absorbed into the NCB in 1947, although the company's own locomotives continued to shunt the docks themselves. When we visited there was a mixed fleet of 0-4-0STs, including *18*, the well-known Lewin of *c*.1875, and several by HL and RSH including HL3496 *B No. 38* and RSH7347 *183*; the HL and RSH locos had come from a variety of sources, including the Consett Iron Co. and Dorman Long and in addition many had cut-down cabs and boiler mountings.

Lewin/c1875, Seaham Harbour Dock Co., *18*. 25 September 1964.

HL3496, Seaham Harbour Dock Co., *B No. 38*. 25 September 1964.

RSH7347, Seaham
Harbour Dock Co., *183*. 25
September 1964.

A visit was made to NCB Philadelphia where 0-6-0PT LEW/1958 No. 6 was being broken up – this engine was a 'bitsa' constructed locally using parts from the withdrawn locos No. 6; a RS 0-6-0 built in 1864, No. 8; another RS 0-6-0 built in 1864, and No. 39; a 0-6-0 ST RWH1422. NCB Springwell Bank Foot had a fleet of six-wheeled tank locomotives for hauling the loads to Monckton Washery and Jarrow Staithes, amongst these was 0-6-0ST HL2545 *24 13,* the steam locos were replaced from 1964 onwards by Diesels by S and HC.

LEW/1958, NCB, Philadelphia, 6, 25 September 1964.

HL2545, NCB, Springwell, *24 13. 25* September 1964.

A visit was also made to NCB Ravensworth Colliery where the NER 0-4-0T Ghd38 No. 64 (1310) was seen but not photographed, this particular engine was later preserved.

The following day, 26 September, we were in Northumberland visiting, amongst other sites, CEGB Blyth Generating Station where 0-4-0ST HL3090 and 0-6-0ST HC1674 *19* were out of use having been replaced by diesel shunters. One of the collieries we visited was NCB Backworth, which provided locos to different collieries as well as services to the staithes at Percy Main. No photographs were taken there, although we were to see 0-6-0ST HC555 *11*, formerly Port Talbot Railway *26* and GWR *813*; this of course was a loco that was preserved and has been restored to working condition. NCB Whittle was also visited, where 0-4-0ST HL3741 *19* was present having recently been repainted at Ashington ACW. At NCB Ashington a large number of locos were present since it served a number of nearby collieries as well as providing a passenger service for colliers; we were shown the aged passenger stock but were advised not to go into the compartments. Amongst the engines seen at Ashington were 0-6-0Ts HC1825 *28*, HL3392 *13*, RSH7609 *31* and RSH7764 *39*, plus 0-6-0STs RSH7104 *44* fitted with a Giesl Ejector, RSH7762 *37* and WB2780 *52*.

At NCB New Biggin 0-6-0ST AE2000 *1* was waiting to be broken up. The former NCBOE site at Widdrington was being operated by Derek Crouch (Contractors) Ltd; amongst their small fleet were 0-6-0STs AB2212 the former LNER J94 Class No. 68078, and HC1539 *Derek Crouch*, which later was purchased for preservation.

HC1674, CEGB,
Blyth, *19*.
26 September 1964.

RSH7104, NCB,
Ashington, *44*.
26 September 1964.

HC1825, NCB,
Ashington, *28*.
26 September 1964.

RSH7764, NCB, Ashington, 39. 26 September 1964.

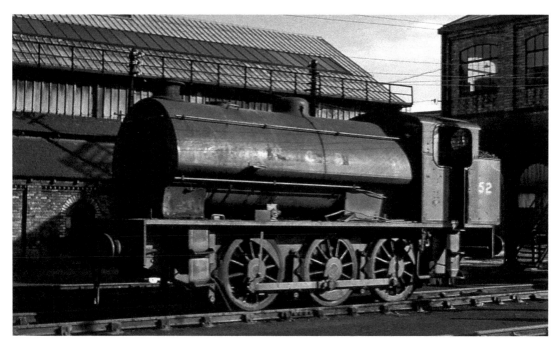

WB2780, NCB, Ashington, 52. 26 September 1964.

Our final visit for the day was to NCB Burradon where 0-4-0ST HL3541 *No. 25* was posing in the evening sunlight in front of the colliery slagheap.

On 27 September we continued our visits to NCB sites in Durham. Seen at Derwenthaugh, which mainly served the local coking plant and staithes, was 0-4-0ST AB970 *61 Derwent* and two withdrawn 4wVBTs S9583 *87* and S9581 *No. 89*. Also visited was NCB Morrison Busty, where 0-6-0ST RSH7641 *No. 84* and the apparently withdrawn 0-6-0ST BH971 *No. 38* was photographed.

AE2000, NCB,
New Biggin, *1*.
26 September 1964.

HC1539, NCBOE, Widdrington, *Derek Crouch*. 26 September 1964.

HL3541, NCB,
Burradon, No. 25.
26 September 1964.

AB970, NCB,
Derwenthaugh,
61 Derwent.
27 September 1964.

S9581, NCB,
Derwenthaugh, 89. 27
September 1964.

BH971, NCB, Morrison Busty, *38*. 27 September 1964.

RSH7641, NCB, Morrison Busty, *84*. 27 September 1964.

A major NCB shed was at Marley Hill, this serviced the western end of the former Bowes Railway, where a new shed building had been built. Amongst the locos in the open that were seen were 0-6-0STs HE3688 No. 20 and HL3103 No. 11. Marley Hill subsequently became the site of the North of England Open Air Museum. After our final visit I remained in Newcastle whilst the others from our group returned south.

Having retained our hire car, I was to visit the recently closed Pelaw Main Staithes loco shed at Bill Quay. The site was being demolished; however the two cut-down locos 0-4-0T HL2986 *69 Charles Perkins* and 0-4-0ST AB786 *62 Tyne* were waiting their

HE3688, NCB,
Marley Hill, No. 20.
27 September 1964.

HL3103, NCB, Marley
Hill, No. 11. 27
September 1964.

fate – sadly, they were not in a suitable position for photography. My final visit was to
NCB Barton Mill, a drift mine situated adjacent to the Newcastle to Carlisle line. There
were two 0-4-0STs seen here BH1068 No. 1 and MW1999 *No. 23*; I was fortunate to
see these two locos since both were broken up in October.

On 17 October LCGB organised at visit to the public utility sites in the Waddon
Marsh area. At SEGB Waddon Marsh the three steam locomotives, 0-4-0STs KS4167
Moss Bay, AE1865 *Elizabeth* and 4wVBT S7109 were lined up together and later
separated so that individual photographs could be taken. Further along the line CEGB
Croydon 'B' Power Station was visited. Here the three cut-down Peckett 0-4-0STs
P2103, P2104 and P2105 were evident. These were built in 1948 and returned to
P pending the completion of the power station and, when returned, had new works
plates dated 1950 fitted.

14 November found our small group at BSC Ipswich where the sole steam loco, 0-6-0ST
P2000 was seen. Other BSC factories visited that weekend were South Lynn, where

MW1999,
NCB, Bardon
Mill, *No. 23*.
28 September 1964.

KS4167, SEGB, Waddon Marsh, *Moss Bay*. 17 October 1964.

S7109, SEGB,
Waddon Marsh, *Joyce*.
17 October 1964.

P2103, CEGB,
Croydon B Power
Station. 17 October
1964.

P2000, BSC, Ipswich.
14 November 1964.

0-6-0STs HC1669 and AE1945 were present, and Wissington, where four 0-6-0STs; AB1931 *BSC No. 2*, MW2004, MW1532 *Newcastle* and HC1700 *15 Wissington* were present. Richard Garratt's of Leiston were noted for traction engines, however their sole loco at that time came from a rival company, 4wWTG AP6158 *Sirapite*. The only other visit on this day was to Barrington Cement Works where the only steam loco was the shortly to be scrapped 0-6-0ST YE2142.

I am not too sure of all the places we visited on 15 November. We certainly went to Byfield Ironstone Co., Crosby, where 0-6-0ST MW1966 *Beauchamp* looked forlorn. However the other two 0-6-0STs HC1630 and HC1366 *Renishaw Ironworks No. 6* appeared to be in fine fettle. At G&T Earle, Kirton Lindsay, the immaculate 0-6-0ST P1939 *Claude* was in steam alongside the Brigg to Gainsborough main line; also present was another 0-6-0ST AB2038 *Cuthbert*. BSC Frodingham Ironstone Mines, Scunthorpe, was the home to a number of 'Austerity' 0-6-0STs including HC1758 *No. 16*, WB2762 *No. 18*, YE2566 *No. 22*, YE2563 *No. 20*, YE2570 *No. 23*, YE2571 *No. 24* and YE2572 *No. 25*.

YE2142, Barrington
Cement Works.
14 November 1964.

MW1966, Byfield
Ironstone, Scunthorpe
Mines, *Beauchamp*.
15 November 1966.

P1939, G&T Earle Ltd, Kirton Lindsay, *Claude*. 15 November 1964.

YE2566, *No. 22* and HC1758 *No. 16* USC Scunthorpe. 15 November 1964.

On 16 November we were back in ironstone country, concentrating on workings in the quarries themselves, fortunately having been advised where best to see locos in action. At SDSI Storefield 0-4-0STs P1289 *Cockspur* and AB2101 *No. 19* were very much in steam. At one of the quarry faces a large seemingly abandoned steam navvy was present. S&L Minerals, Wellingborough, was a metre gauge system with three large 0-6-0STs P1870 *No. 85*, P1871 *No. 86* and P2029 *No. 87* – we were to see P1871 being loaded at the quarry face.

P1289, SDSI, Storefield, *Cockspur.* 16 November 1964.

AB2101, SDSI, Storefield, *No. 19.* 16 November 1964.

Steam Navvy, SDSI, Storefield. 16 November 1964.

P1871, S&L Mineral, Wellingborough, *No. 86* at the quarry face. 16 November 1964.

Finally, a visit was made to the quarries at Corby. This was an extensive system, in part double track and colour light signals, and because of the weight of some of the loads involved locos were positioned at the front and rear of the trains. An example of this was RSH7672 *61* being banked by RSH7673 *62*. Other 0-6-0STs seen working included K5473 *46 Cardigan*, RSH7004 *52*, RSH7668 *57* and RSH7030 *53*. At the steelworks interchange sidings HL3375 *40* was again seen, together with the second Shanks & McEwan 0-4-0ST P2026 *C57 T. S. Wilson*.

On 28 November the North West Branch of LCGB organised a visit to Trafford Park, Manchester. At Brown & Polson 0-4-0ST AB1964 was present. Proctor & Gamble's 0-4-0F AB1467 was also seen. Also seen were the two 0-4-0STs at Turners Asbestos, HL2645 *Turnall* and HL2780 *Asbestos*.

RSH7004, S&L
Minerals, Corby, *52*.
16 November 1964.

RSH7672, S&L
Minerals, Corby, *61*
with RSH7673 *62* out
of sight at the rear.
16 November 1964.

AB1964, Brown &
Polson, Trafford Park.
28 November 1964.

AB1467, Proctor &
Gamble, Trafford Park.
28 November 1964.

HL2645, Turners Asbestos,
Trafford Park *Turnall*.
28 November 1964.

The final visit was to MSC Mode Wheel. The line itself ran from Ellesmere Port in the west, alongside the Canal to Manchester Trafford Park in the east, and at its peak there were some 231 miles of track and sidings. The locomotive fleet by the time of my visit comprised two classes of 0-6-0Ts from HC, the earlier ones having shorter side tanks, 0-6-0Ts from K with side tanks, which extended to the smokebox door similar to the long tank engines from HC, plus a couple of 'Austerity' 0-6-0STs from HC waiting to be scrapped. From 1959 onward a number of 0-6-0 diesel locomotives had been purchased from HC, and later S and RR, these were gradually replacing the fleet of steam locos. The HC locos delivered before 1914 were originally only named, although between 1914 and 1915 numbers were allocated and the nameplates removed, one being positioned inside the cab; hearsay has it this was because *Hamburg*, later *31*, had been stoned by patriotic dock workers in the early days of the First World War. On this visit I was to photograph four short tank engines, known as 'Jazzers'; HC663 *30*, HC740 *39*, HC775 *44* and HC799 *51*, as well as two 'long tankers' HC1240 *64* and HC1361 *65*.

This completed a first, interesting, year searching for industrial steam.

HC663, MSC,
Mode Wheel *30*.
28 November 1964.

HC1361, MSC
Mode Wheel *65*.
8 November 1964.

Chapter Three

1965 – Visits to Wales, Scotland and Many Other Places

Early in January 1965 I had been mainline spotting in Scotland. On the way back south I stopped off, as one does, in County Durham, so on 8 January a few industrial visits were made. At NCB Hylton two 0-4-0STs were present RSH7414 *7* and RSH7804 *8*. Nearby was NCB Wearmouth, where 0-6-0ST RSH7689 *3* and 0-6-0T HL2769 *Jean* were both at work preparing freights to be taken away by a Q6 0-8-0. Finally I managed to take a photograph over the wall at Doxford & Sunderland Shipbuilding, Pallion, of 0-4-0CT RSH7070 *Millfield*, one of five crane tanks here. I was to make an official visit to Pallion at a later date when we were advised photography was not permitted.

RSH7414, NCB Hylton 7. 8 January 1964.

HL2769, NCB, Wearmouth, *Jean*. 8 January 1965.

RSH7689, NCB, Wearmouth, *3*. 8 January 1965.

RSH7070, Doxford & Sunderland Shipbuilding, Pallion, Sunderland, *Millfield*. 8 January 1964.

On 23 January we left in pretty miserable weather by car to South Wales to visit some NCB Collieries; this was the weekend when Sir Winston Churchill died so, although not music lovers, there was only restricted interest on the car radio. A full list of the collieries visited has been lost in the passage of time, but photographic records show we went to NCB Bedwas where 0-6-0ST AB1091 *Lundie* was in steam; 0-6-0ST HL3923 *58* was at NCB Celynen North; four locos were seen at NCB Celynen South, 0-4-0ST AB1011 *Joan No. 12A*, 0-6-0STs P1889 *Menelaus* and RSH7800 *No. 47*. At Nantgawr Coke Plant there were three 'Austerity' 0-6-0STs HE3767 *No. 1*, HE3768 *No. 2* and HE3687 *No. 3*. Finally, in the snow at NCB Ogilvie there were two 0-6-0STs HC1738 and WB2995 *402*.

HL3923, NCB
Celynen North *58*.
23 January 1965.

WB2995, NCB Ogilvie *402*. 23 January 1965.

HE3768, NCB Nantgarw Coke Plant *No. 1*. 23 January 1965.

After the collieries we made nocturnal visits to some of the Western Region loco sheds (which ones I do not recall) where there were a number of 'dead' 5600 class 0-6-2Ts. I do not have a log of the actual engine numbers but thanks to Swindon's brass plates we were able to get their details. It really is a shame all my individual records were lost.

More collieries were visited the following day (24 January), of which only two photographs were taken. At NCB Merthyr Vale there were two 0-6-0STs P2061 *No. 6* and the veteran HC543 *9*. At Aberaman 0-6-0ST HC606 *7* was waiting its fate having been replaced by former GWR 0-6-0 PT *9762*.

P2061, NCB Merthyr Vale *No. 6*. 24 January 1965.

Sdn/1936, NCB
Aberaman 9762.
24 January 1965.

HC606, NCB
Aberaman 7.
24 January 1965.

I know we must have visited Blaenavon since I can still recall driving over the mountain in snow and ice; one of the locos there, 0-6-0ST HE3810 *Glendower*, is in an incomplete list of sighting. Using that list it would appear we also went to Aberpengw, Banwen, Bargoed, Caerphilly Tar Works, Cefn Coed, Duffryn Rhonna, Felin Fran, Garngoch, Graig Merthyr, Groesfaen, Marine, Mountain Ash, Nine Mile Point, Penrikyber, Risca, Taff Merthyr, Tower, NCBOE Glyn Neath and NCBOE Gwaun Cae Gurwen. I was to make a later visit to South Wales in July 1965 but think that was mainly to Steel Works, but could have included some of those collieries.

A visit to Derbyshire commenced on 13 February 1965. Two NCB Collieries were visited; Morton where 0-4-0ST P1254 *Jubilee* was present, and Ramcroft, which had 0-4-0ST AE1999 *David* on view. The Ironworks at Sheepbridge were also visited. Two 0-6-0STs were here; HC1023 *24* and, abandoned in a derelict part of the works, HC248 *No. 21*. However the best visit of the day was to Bourne & Shaw, Wirksworth, where both of their 0-4-0STs, BH266 No. 3 and P1257 *Uppingham*, were in steam and positioned for photographs. Both of these popular locomotives were later preserved.

AE1999, NCB,
Ramcroft, *David*.
13 February 1965.

P1254, NCB, Morton, *Jubilee.* 13 February 1965.

HC1023, Sheepbridge Ironworks, *No. 24.* 13 February 1965.

HC248, Sheepbridge
Ironworks, *No. 21.*
13 February 1965.

BH266, Bourne & Shaw,
Wirksworth, *Holwell No. 3.*
13 February 1965.

P1275, Bourne & Shaw,
Wirksworth, *Uppingham*
and BH266 *Holwell No. 3.*
13 February 1965.

Visits were made on 14 February to NCB Bentinck, where photographs were taken of 0-6-0ST YE2197 *Bentinck No.3*, 0-4-0ST HL2657 *Daisy* and 0-6-0T HC1878 *Emfour 3* – one of several to the same specification order by that NCB Division. Another of the HC tanks, HC1877 *Emfour 2* was seen at NBC Brookhall, whereas at NCB Coppice 0-6-0ST HE1470 *26*, another more or less standard design, stood in the yard. Many NCB Areas purchased 100 h.p. 4wVBT locos from S – S9397 *Bonnie Dundee* at NCB Kirkby was an example.

HC1878, NCB, Bentinck, *Emfour 3*. 14 February 1965.

YE2197, NCB, Bentinck, *Bentinck No. 3*. 14 February 1965.

HL2657, NCB, Bentinck, *Daisy*. 14 February 1965.

HE1470, NCB, Coppice, 26. 14 February 1965.

S9397, NCB, Kirkby, *Bonnie Dundee*. 14 February 1965.

Surplus War Department 'Austerity' 0-6-0ST, designed by HE and built by a number of other manufacturers, were bought by the NCB. Included amongst them were VF5286 *36* at Moor Green and WB2754 at NCBOE West Hallam, still bearing its old WD number 75166. At NCB Pye Hill the cut down 0-4-0ST AB1010 *No. 12* was in a compound, and finally at NCB Winning 'A' there was the attractive 0-4-0ST P1503.

AB1010, NCB, Pye Hill, *No. 12*. 14 February 1965.

P1503, NCB, Winning 'A'. 14 February 1965.

Mention has to be made of the two unique Markham & Co. 0-4-0STs seen. Mkm *109 Charles* at NCB Markham Main and Mkm *112* at Geo.Slate Ltd, Beighton. *No. 3*, Mkm *109*, should now be found at Butterley.

I was in a party of people on 20 March who visited Gloucestershire and other locations. This was a trip where I took very few photographs and do not recall many of the places we went to. One most certainly was CEGB Gloucester to see their 0-4-0F AB2126.

AB2126, CEGB, Gloucester. 20 March 1965.

Other places I know we visited included J. S. Fry & Co., Somerdale, where 4wVBT S7492 was present; most impressive was the original vertical works plate with a sentinel leaning on his sword. SWGB Cheltenham had the former Port of Bristol 0-6-0ST P2035 *S10 Hallen* – the only steam locomotive present. Fred Watkins, Milkwall, was a plant dealer and 0-4-0ST WB2648 *ROF 18 No. 2* was waiting a new purchaser. I feel that we also visited the NCB collieries at Kilmersdon, 0-4-0ST P1788, and Norton Hill HE1684.

Returning eastwards on 21 March a visit was made to Roads Reconstruction, Vobster, where just a single loco was present; S9374 *781 1* – a 100 h.p. loco to the same design as the engines bought in some numbers by NCB. Finally in the Southampton area the following firms were visited: Burt, Boulton & Haywood 0-4-0ST AB1299 *Benton II*; SGB Southampton, the Chapel Tramway, 0-4-0ST AB1398, P. D. Fuels, Northiam, 0-4-0ST P2128, 0-4-0ST RSH7544 *Bonnie Prince Charlie*, and 0-4-0T 9E/1893 No. 30096 *Corrall Queen* were all present.

3 April saw a visit to CEGB Earley Power Station near Reading. There were two 0-4-0STs there; RSH7058 and RSH7306, together with 4wDM MR3966 looking like a mobile glass house.

S9374, Roads ReConstruction Vobster *781 1*. 21 March 1965.

RSH7544, PD Fuels, Hamworthy, *Bonnie Prince Charlie*. 21 March 1965.

MR3966, CEGB, Earley, No. 3. 3 April 1965.

RSH 7306, CEGB, Earley. 3 April 1965.

I am certain we would have gone to the nearby Huntley & Palmers biscuit factory, although I could well have seen their two 0-4-0 Fs, WB2473 No. 1 and WB2474 No. 2, at some stage when passing by on a train. We most certainly went to Slough Estates and saw their two 0-6-0 STs, HC1544 No. 3 and HC1709 No. 5.

A group visit to Scotland commenced on 16 April. I recall that I was in Edinburgh the day before to collect a minibus, which had to be returned since it was too small and not fit for purpose. Instead we had a Bedford Dormobile – not the best of vehicles from a driving point of view. This visit was to go to a number of places over four days, and whilst I do not have individual dates, unlike other group travels, I was to later mark sighting in my copy of the IRS Scotland Handbook. The following list is in alphabetic order of where we went. From my lists of photographs taken the date of visit is also shown:

Bairds & Scottish Steel Ltd Gartsherrie, Coatbridge. 0-4-0STs N3629 *No. 3*, N3994 *No. 5*, NBL16732 *No. 7* and NBL18385 *No. 19*.

Bairds and Scottish Steel Ltd Northburn. 0-4-0STs AB1467 *No. 4*, AB1508 *No. 5*, N3629 *No. 3* and NR5566.

Wm. Beardmore & Co. Parkhead Forge. 0-4-0ST AB2253 *No. 6*.

BP Grangemouth. 0-6-0F AB1552 *No. 1* (visit was on 19 April).

British Aluminium, Burntisland. 0-4-0STs P1376, P1579 *No. 2* and AB2046 *No. 3* (visit was on 19 April).

Carron Co. Carron Ironworks, Falkirk. 0-4-0STs AB1781 *No. 15*, AB1798 *No. 6* and WB2677 *No. 10*.

Colvilles Ltd Clyde Ironworks, Tollcross. 0-4-0STs AB2133 *No. 11* and AB2120 *No. 12*.

Colvilles Ltd Clydebridge. 0-4-0CT AB1504 *No. 2*, 0-4-0STs HL3166 *No. 4*, HL3736 *No. 8*, RSH7081, and 4wVBT S9620 *2/19* (visit was on 16 April).

Colvilles Ltd Dalzell Iron & Steel Works. 0-4-0CT AB838, 0-4-0STs P1474 *No. 29* and HC1303 *33* (visit was on 16 April).

Colvilles Ltd Mossend Engineering Works. 0-4-0STs AE1779 *No. 2* and P614 *No. 3*.

Culter Paper Mills, Peterculter. 0-4-0ST P1998.

Dailuaine-Talisker Distillery, Dailuaine. 0-4-0ST AB2073 *Dailuiane* (visit was on 17 April).

ICI Ltd Mossend. 0-4-0ST RSH7052.

Lanarkshire Steel Co. Ltd Craigneuk. 0-4-0STs AB2161 *1* and AB2194 *No. 4*.

R. & Y. Pickering, Wishaw. 0-4-0ST RWH2009 *No. 3* (visit was on 16 April).

ScGB Aberdeen. 0-4-0STs BH912 *City of Aberdeen*, AB807 *Bon Accord*, AB1889 *No. 3* and AB2239 *No. 4 Mr Therm* (visit was on 17 April).

ScGB Granton. 0-4-0STs AB1967 *6* and AB1890 *10*, plus 3 foot gauge 0-4-0T AB1871 *9*.

Scottish Malt Distillery, Balmenach. 0-4-0ST AB2020.

S. & L. Clydesdale Steel and Tubes Works, Mossend. 0-4-0STs AB2223 *Clydesdale No. 13*, AB2286 *Mossend No. 13* and RSH7057 *No. 5*.

S. & L. Tollcross. 0-4-0ST AB2163 *Seamless*.

R. B. Tennent Ltd, Whefflet Foundry, nr. Coatbridge. 4wVBT S9628 *Robin*, S9561 *John* and S9631 *Denis*.

TPCM Gartsherrie. 0-4-0ST NBL16732 *No. 7*.

T. W. Ward, Long Loan Wagon Repair Depot, Coatbridge. 0-4-0ST P1326 No. 4.

T. W. Ward, Inverkeithing. 0-4-0STs P1738 *TW2568* and AB2081 *No. 4 Marlborough* (visit was on 17 April).

Wemyss Private Railway, Dysart. 0-6-0STs HE2888 *No. 14*, AB2183. *No. 15* and WB2759 *No. 16*. 0-6-0Ts AB2017 *No. 17*, AB2048 *No. 18*, AB2067 *No. 19*, AB2068 *No. 20* (visit was on 18 April).

NCB Bowhill. 0-4-0STs AB1339 *No. 2* and *No. 56* (visit was on 17 April).

NCB Comrie. 0-6-0STs AB2257 *No. 33* and WB2777.

NCB Cowdenbeath Central Workshops. 0-4-0STs AB2113 *No. 16*, AB642 *No. 8*, GR146 *No. 20*, GR427 *No. 15*, AB1825 *No. 36*, AB1125 *No. 43*, AB727 *No. 24* and AB2206 *No. 19*.

NCB Cowdenbeath No. 7. 0-4-0ST AB910 *No. 54*.

NCB Frances. 0-4-0ST AB2357 *No. 20* (visit was on 17 April).

NCB Frances Shops. 0-4-0ST AB975 *No. 5*, Giesl ejector fitted 0-6-0T AB1297 *No. 8* (visit was on 17 April).

NCB Glengraig. 0-4-0STs AB1107 *No. 41*, AB1289 *No. 39* and AB899 *No. 48*.

NCB Kinneil. 0-4-0STs AB2259 *No. 4*, AB1981 *No. 5* and GR480 *No. 31*.

NCB Kinglassie. 0-4-0ST AB1125 *No. 34*.

NCB Manor Powis. 0-4-0STs AB974 *No. 11* and AB1740.

NCB Mary. 0-4-0STs AB898 *No. 49* and AB1291 *No. 42*.

NCB Michael. 0-4-0ST AB2262 *No. 7*, 0-6-0STs RSH7109 *No. 13* and HE3837 (visit was on 17 April)

NCB Minto. 0-4-0STs AB1283 *No. 37* and AB1291 *No. 42*.

NCB Nellie. 0-4-0STs AB1146 *No. 62* and AB2261 *No. 6* (visit was on 17 April)

NCB Valleyfield. 0-4-0STs AB1657 *No. 60* and AB1807 *No. 53*.

NCB Wellesley. 0-6-0STs AB764 *No. 1*, NBL16154 *No. 4*, NBL16463 *No. 7* and AB1245 *No. 10* (visit was on 18 April).

NCBOE Westfield. 0-6-0STs HE3194 *75141 WL No. 1*, HE3187 *75147 WL No. 3* and Hunslet Underfeed Stoker fitted HE3185 *75135 WL No. 2* (visit was on 18 April).

AB1552, B. P. Refinery,
Grangemouth, *No. 1.*
19 April 1965.

P1376, British Aluminium,
Burntisland. 19 April 1965.

AB1504, Colvilles Clydesdale,
No. 2. 16 April 1965.

AB838, Colvilles Dalzell,
No. 14. 16 April 1965.

P1474, Colville Dalzell,
No. 29. 16 April 1965.

AB2073, Dailuaine
Distillery, Nr. Aberlour,
No. 1 Dailuaine.
17 April 1965.

RWH2009, R&Y Pickering, Wishaw, *No. 3.* 16 April 1965.

AB1889, ScGB, Aberdeen, *No. 3.* 17 April 1965.

BH912, ScGB, Aberdeen, *City of Aberdeen.* 17 April 1965.

AB2081, T. W. Ward
Inverkeithing *No. 4*
Marlborough. 17 April 1965

WB2759, *WPR No. 16.*
18 April 1965.

AB1339, NCB, Bowhill, *No. 2.*
17 April 1965.

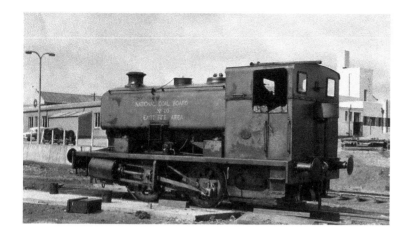

AB2357, NCB, Frances
Colliery, *No. 20.*
17 April 1965.

AB1297, NBC,
Frances Shops, *No. 8.*
17 April 1965.

AB2262, NCB, *Michael*
No. 7. 17 April 1965.

AB2261, NCB, Nellie,
No. 6. 17 April 1965.

NBL16463, NCB, Wellesley,
No. 7. 18 April 1965.

HE3185, NCBOE,
Westfield *75135 WL No. 2.*
18 April 1965.

It is possible we also visited British Aluminium, Fort William, since I have a note of seeing the two 3 foot gauge 0-4-2STs KS3024 *No. 1 Sir Murray Morrison* and HE1842 *No. 2 Lady Morrison* possibly prior to preservation.

The intention of this detailed list is to demonstrate the scope of locomotives to be seen at the time on extended trips. Many of the locations also had diesel locomotives, for which I do not have details.

After the extended Scottish tour the next visits started 6 June when we were in Cumbria. One of the places we went to was NCB Harrington, where 0-6-0STs VF5304 *9229/3* and VF5282 *WD187* were present as well as 0-6-0T HL3466 *No. 5* and the last of their inside cylinder 0-4-0T P1107 *MillGrove*. The final colliery we went to was NCB St Helens where 0-4-0STs AE1729, AE1777 *Askham Hall* and YE2431 *St. Helens No. 2* were present as well as 0-6-0ST AB1817 *Oak Lea*. At Workington Harbour & Dock Co. there were four 0-4-0STs; YE2425 *No. 1*, YE2429 *No. 17*, YE2585 *No. 18* and YE2587 *No. 19*.

The main visit of the day was to Workington Iron & Steel Works, Moss Bay. Here there were a number of 0-6-0STs; RS4087 *No. 58*, RS4088 *No. 59*, RS4142 *No. 60*, RSH7061 *No. 61*, RSH7666 *No. 68*, RSH7750 *No. 71* and RSH7946 *No. 78*. There were five 0-4-0STs; AB2159 *No. 62*, AB2203 *No. 65*, AB2236 *No. 66*, YE2602 *No. 70* and RSH7048 *No. 73*. Also seen was 4wWE HL3856 working at the coke ovens.

We were to visit CEGB Willow Holme Power Station in Carlisle on June 7 where three 0-6-0 Fs were present; AB1488 *No. 1*, AB2153 *No. 2* and AB2193 *No. 3*. At Carrs of Carlisle their single 0-4-0F AB1435 *Despatch*, resplendent in Caledonian Railway blue livery, was photographed. On our way south and east we were to see 0-4-0DM JF411203 at Shap Granite, 0-4-0ST AB2343 at British Gypsum, Kirkby Thore, and 0-4-0ST HC1546 at Acrow Granite.

YE2429, Workington Harbour, No. 17. 6 June 1965.

RS4142, WIS, Moss Bay,
Workington, *No. 60*.
6 June 1965.

RSH7750, *No. 71*, WIS,
Moss Bay, Workington.
6 June 1965.

AB1435, Carr of
Carlisle Ltd, *Despatch*.
6 June 1965.

AB2343, British Gypsum, Kirkby Thore. 7 June 1965.

I was to experience one of the problems of being a group leader at Sir Hedworth Williamson Ltd, at Kirkby Stephen. Both of their locos – 0-4-0STs HL3890 *Helen* and HL3806 *Billy* – had their nameplates and builder's plates removed and placed against the wall inside the sheds. Two members of the party with larger bags than the rest of us decided these plates would make good trophies until I intervened. I think at the start of this trip I must have hired our transport in Leeds since that is where I dropped the party off after travelling through the Yorkshire Dales, stopping off in Wensleydale to buy some local cheeses.

Most of the trips we did by road. I had a navigator to direct me where to go since in the days before sat navs it was either local knowledge or maps, which I obviously could not use and drive at the same time. It must therefore follow that my navigator must have stayed with me on 8 June when we went to Brookes of Lightcliffe to see their three 0-6-0STs; P1830 *Silex No. 2*, P2160 *Nonslip Stone* and HE2387 *No. 1* looking as if it needed a good clean. HC1882 *Mirvale* was at Mirvale Chemicals, Mirfield. Finally, looking over a wall, KS2391 *David Fulton* appeared to be very much out of use at Yorkshire Tar Distillers, Cleckheaton.

After a very short break on 10 June we were again back in ironstone country photographing some of the workings. At Corby Minerals we were to photograph 0-6-0STs MW1762 *38 Dolobran* and three of the later locos built by Kitson to the same design, K5470 *45 Colwyn*, K5473 *46 Cardigan* and K5476 *48 Criggon*. Also seen were two of the larger RSH locos; RSH7670 *59* and RSH7761 *63*. In the main this fleet of sturdy steam locos were later replaced by redundant Swindon built Class 14 (D95xx) 0-6-0DHs.

HE2387, Brookes,
Lightbridge, *No. 1*.
8 June 1965.

HC1882, Mirvale
Chemicals, Mirfield,
Mirvale. 8 June 1965.

KS2391, Yorkshire
Tar Distillers,
Cleckheaton, *David
Fulton*. 8 June 1965.

K5470, S&L
Minerals,
Corby 45
Colwyn.
10 June 1965.

K5476, S&L
Minerals,
Corby 48
Criggon.
10 June 1965.

MW1762,
S&L Minerals,
Corby 38
Dolobran.
10 June 1965.

The other working quarry that we visited was SDSI Irchester. The diminutive 0-4-0ST MW1795 *No. 14* was running alongside a water-filled dyke overshadowed by the large trucks it was hauling. The much larger 0-4-0ST HL3780 *Holwell No. 3* showed it was capable of taking a much heavier load, as was 0-6-0ST AB1497 *No. 6*.

MW1795, SDSI, Irchester *No. 14.* 10 June 1965.

AB1497, SDSI, Irchester *No. 6.* 10 June 1965.

A weekend group visit to some of the iron and steel works in South Wales, plus some other places thrown in, began on 10 July. Many of those visited closed before the Nationalisation of the iron and steel industry in July 1968. The only place where I took any photographs was Llanelli Steel Co. Ltd Llanelly Steel Works where several 0-4-0STs were present including the cut down inside cylindered AB1276 *No. 3 Nora* and AB1277 *No. 4 Lindsay*, which was being used in the Melting Shops. There were also ten conventional outside cylindered 0-4-0STs present, some of which were evidently no longer in use.

Other iron and steel works visited included RTB Elba Steel Works, Gowerton, where six Peckett 0-4-0STs were seen, again several of which were out of use including P1071 *Brunel*. A few months after our visit I received a letter from the works manager thanking us for our interest in this particular loco and, since it was scheduled to be scrapped, were there any parts that we would like to have. Rather in hope than expectation I suggested perhaps a nameplate or builder's plate. To my surprise a large wooden box was delivered to my home with one of each plate, the nameplate is now in my porch and I swapped the works plate for another with LCGB.

AB1277, Llanelli Steel, *No. 4*, *Lindsay*. 10 July 1965.

Nameplate P1071, *Brunel*, ex-RTB Elba.

Some of the other places visited were Briton Ferry Steel Co., Albion Works, which had five 0-4-0STs; two by BP and three by P. Stephens Silica Brick Co. Kidwelly Brickworks had 0-4-0ST P2082 *Sir Alfred*. Also in the Kidwelly area was the plant works of J. P. Zammit Ltd. Although there was no rail traffic, stored in its shed was FW410 *Margaret*, which had been there since 1942 when the previous Kidwelly Tinplate Co. had closed down. It had arrived in 1923 from the GWR numbered 1378 having been absorbed from the Gwendraeth Valley Railway where it was their *No. 2*. Thankfully this historic locomotive was saved for preservation and can now be seen at the Pembrokeshire County Council Museum near Haverfordwest.

On 17 July we must have been working in the morning since the first of two visits in Kent did not take place until the afternoon. We were to visit Empire Paper Mills at Greenhithe where their two 0-4-0Fs had been augmented by 0-4-0ST P1880 *Nelson*. The other visit was to Imperial Paper, Gravesend, where their four 0-4-0Fs; OK4708 *Marion*, OK5900 *No. 2*, AB2373 *Imperial No. 1* and AB1496 *No. 2* were present.

OK5900, Imperial Paper Mills, Gravesend, *No. 2*. 17 July 1965.

On the 18 July visits were made to the Kent Coalfields. At NCB Chislet 0-6-0STs HC1495 *No. 1 St Augustine* and YE2498 were seen as well as 0-4-0 ST P2156 in silver undercoat, being repainted. NCB Betteshanger had three 0-6-0STs; HE3825 *No. 9*, HE3827 *No. 10* and the slightly smaller YE2448 *No. 11*. Finally at NCB Snowdown 0-6-0STs AE1971 *St Thomas* and AE2004 *St Dunstan* were present. APCM Swanscombe was also visited. Here they had a fleet of seven 0-4-0STs to the same design by HL and RSH. Although numbered from No. 1 to No. 7 – with the numbers on the tanks – the actual number shown did not always match up with the original numbers due to the saddle tanks being swapped at times.

This was to prove to be my last industrial visit in 1965. In September I took up a job with the British Railways Board in Leeds which effectively restricted my photographic forays for the rest of the year.

P2156, NCB Chislet. 18 July 1965.

HL3715, APCM
Swanscombe,
No. 1.
18 July 1965.

HL3715, *No. 1* and RSH7405, *No. 7*, APCM, Swanscombe. 18 July 1965.

Chapter Four

1966 – A Period Mainly in the Northern Half of England

On 12 March the North West Branch of LCGB arranged a series of open wagon trips along the lines of Cooke & Nuttall Ltd, Black Rod near Horwich, hauled by their 0-4-0ST AB2230 *Douglas*, which included run pasts, etc. Also visited on that day was Thos. Walmsey & Sons at Bolton where their similar 0-4-0ST AB1882 *Atherton* was in steam for us.

A visit to Chatham Dockyard with LCGB was made on 12 April, where some of their locos were positioned just inside the entrance gateway, was made. My recollection is that we actually saw very many of the fleet of five 0-4-0STs and seven 4wDMs; certainly 0-4-0ST RSH7042 *S. Y. S. Yard No. 361 Ajax* was present together with two of the three AB 0-4-0STs. Also seen was 4wDH *Yard No. 562 Deal Castle*.

AB2230, Cooke & Nuttall, Horwich, *Douglas*. 12 March 1966.

AB2230, Cooke & Nuttall, Horwich, *Douglas*, working an open wagon tour. 12 March 1966.

AB1882, Thomas Walmsey, Bolton. 12 March 1966.

RSH7042, Chatham Dockyard *S. Y. S. Yard No. 361 Ajax*. 2 April 1966.

AE1648, SEGB, Eastbourne,
Anne. 24 April 1966.

On 24 April I was seconded by LCGB Croydon Branch to help on their Pul/Pan farewell Rail Tour, which ran Victoria–Ore–Eastbourne–Lewes–Seaford–Brighton–Victoria; well, it was a free ride. During the stopover in Eastbourne I was able to visit SEGB Eastbourne, which I had never been to before. Both of their 0-4-0STs; AE1648 *Anne* and AE 1564 *Mary*, were present.

Another series of visits were organised by the North West branch of LCGB, this time on 7 May. Two were CEGB power stations at Agecroft, where 0-4-0STs RSH7416 *No. 1* and RSH7681 were seen, and then to Chadderton for 0-4-0ST AB2367 *No. 2*. No visit to the Manchester area would be complete without going, again, to MSC Mode Wheel. This time I was to photograph 'Jazzer' HC679 *31* – the former *Hamburg* – and long tank HC940 *52*. Also photographed were 0-6-0DE HC D1254 *D10*, 0-6-0DHs S10174 *DH15* and S10193 *DH19*.

RSH7681, CEGB, Agecroft.
7 May 1966.

AB2367, CEGB, Chadderton, *No. 2*. 7 May 1966.

S10174, MSC, Mode Wheel, *DH19*. 7 May 1966.

HC, D1254, MSC, Mode Wheel, *DH10*. 7 May 1966.

HC679, MSC, Mode Wheel, *31*. 7 May 1966.

On 15 June I was persuaded to steward, yet again, on another LCGB Rail Tour, this time to France, however there was a reward the following day – a second visit to Bowaters, Sittingbourne. Save for WB3024, which had departed to Welshpool, all of the stock was seen, many of which were photographed including 0-4-2ST KS1049 *Excelsior*, 0-6-2Ts WB2192 *Conqueror*, WB2624 *Superb* and 2-4-0F WB2216 *Unique*. Also photographed was the former SECR P class 0-6-0T *Pioneer II*.

WB2624, Bowaters, Sittingbourne, *Superb*. 16 May 1966.

P class ex-31178, Bowaters, Sittingbourne, *Pioneer II*. 16 May 1966.

KS1049,
Bowaters,
Sittingbourne,
Excelsior.
16 May 1966.

WB2192, Bowaters, Sittingbourne, *Conqueror*. 16 May 1966.

WB2216, Bowaters, Sittingbourne, *Unique*. 16 May 1966.

There were two IRS group visits organised for 21 May. One was to Naylor Benson, Nassington, where two of their three 0-6-0STs were photographed; P1232 *Buccueth* and HE1982 *Ring Haw*. However the real purpose of the visit was a tour in goods wagons of the system at S&L Pilton, where 0-6-0ST AE1972 *Stamford* did the honours.

AE1972, S&L Minerals, Pilton, *Stamford*, working an open wagon tour. 21 May 1966.

A long weekend visit to the North East started on 28 May with visits to CEGB Stella South to photograph 0-4-0ST RSH7743 *No. 20*, NEGB Elswick for 0-4-0ST RSH7232 *T. P. Ridley*, and Wallsend Slipway to see oil fired 0-4-0WT EB37 *No. 3*. On 29 May we went to a smoky NCB Derwenthaugh Coking Ovens where two 'long boiler' 0-6-0PTs were stabled K2509 *41* and K4295 *5 Major*. These were originally members of Consett Iron Co. class 'A' 0-6-0PTs built to a standard design by HL, K, HC and RSH. On the other side of the Tyne the conditions at NCB Ashington were no better. 0-6-0Ts RSH7609 *31* and RSH7764 *39* and 0-6-0STs P2033 *6*, RSH7178 *27* and WB2750 *49* were all photographed. We seemed to have made only one photographic visit on 30 May, to Blyth Harbour where the remaining steam loco, 0-4-0ST HL2918 *No. 2* appeared to be out of use. We also went to CEGB Stella North and saw 0-4-0ST RSH7795 *23*, 4wVBTs S9595 *24*, and S9597 *25*. At NGB St Anthony's Works there were three 0-4-0STs; HL2704 *Colonel Crawford*, HL3578 *Lt. Colonel W. H. Ritson* and P2142 *Northern Gas Board No.1*. Our final visit was on 31 May to CEGB Dunston, where six locos were present; 0-4-0STs HL3772 *No. 8*, HL3732 *No. 13*, RSH7063 *No. 15* and RSH7679 *No. 17*, 0-6-0ST HC1609 *No. 69* and 0-4-0 DE AW D21 *No. 14*.

On 6 August we were in Essex. The only place visited where photographs were taken was Ford Motor Co. Ltd at Dagenham. By the time of our visit there were just four steam locomotives left; 0-6-0STs P1861 *No. 4*, P1890 *No. 5*, P1938 *No. 7* and P2154 *No. 8*. I am unsure that any of the BTH Bo-BoDEs were still there since all three were disposed of during 1966. Also visited were Thurrock Chalk and Whiting, where two 0-4-0STs, WB2879 *Comet* and P1746 *Southfleet*, were the only remaining steam locos, and TPCC Thurrock, where 0-6-0T P1920 *Coronation* remained.

RSH7743, CEGB, Stella South, *No. 20.* 28 May 1966.

RSH7232, NEGB, Elswick, *T. P. Ridley.* 28 May 1966.

EB37, Wallsend Slipway, *No. 3.* 28 May 1966.

AW D21, CEGB, Dunston, *No. 14.* 30 May 1966.

P2023, NCB, *Ashington 6.* 29 May 1966.

HL2918, Blyth Harbour Commission, *B. H. C. No. 2.* 30 May 1966.

Ford Motor Co., Dagenham, unknown 0-6-0ST by Peckett & Co. 6 August 1966.

It was about this time when I received a letter from the manager at Colvilles Ltd, Mossend, who, in view of the interest shown in P614 during the visit over Easter 1965, asked if they could donate P614 to the LCGB. This was in part due to the pending disposal of assets prior to the nationalisation of the iron and steel industries. After discussing this with the LCGB committee it was decided to accept the offer and I advised Colvilles accordingly. In September I went to Scotland with three objectives in mind. One was to visit Mossend to formally thank the manager there and photograph P614; the second was to go to the Scottish Railway Preservation Society, at that time based at Falkirk, to obtain their agreement to storing P614 before it could be moved south to the Sittingbourne and Kemsley Railway at Sittingbourne; and the third was to visit Andrew Barclay's works at Kilmarnock to look at their engine register to see if there were any details available relating a rebuild they undertook in 1944. Whilst at Kilmarnock I was shown the production line, where a series of diesel shunters were under construction for the MOD. Also seen was their own shunter, AB1219 *Caledonia Works*.

P614, Colvilles, Mossend, *No. 3 Bear*. September 1966.

Although I was living in Leeds I was only to take part in a single further group visit. On 24 September we went to CEGB Mexborough where 0-4-0ST HC1730 *2* was photographed. Seen from outside the buildings at Kirkstall Forge were 0-4-0STs HC1309 *Henry Du Lac II* and HC1716 *Henry Du Lac III*. A visit was made to NCB Frickley where four 0-6-0STs were present; VF5292 *Frickley No. 3*, HE1672 *Frickley No. 4*, HE3593 *Frickley No. 5* and HE3845 *Frickley No. 6*. Several other collieries were also visited over the weekend, the only one I have a positive date for was NCB *Orgreave* on the 25 September. The only steam engine here was 0-6-0T HC1731 *No. 20*. The other collieries we went to were NCB Crigglestone, where 0-4-0ST HC1880 *Fred* was present, and NCB Lofthouse, where 0-6-0STs HC1175 *69* and HC1872 NCB *3 Nineteen Fifty Four* L40950 were seen. Finally at Cohen, Stanningley, there were three 0-4-0STs; HC402, HE1705 *No. 600* and K5037.

HC1730, CEGB,
Mexborough, 2.
24 September 1966.

HE3593, NCB,
Frickley No. 5.
24 September 1966.

HC1731, NCB, *Orgreave No. 20.* 25 September 1966.

My final visit for 1966 was on 1 October to the metre gauge lines at S&L Minerals, Wellingborough. This was a visit organised by either ILS or IRS just prior to the closure of the quarries. Passenger carrying trips were run to and from the quarry face using 0-6-0STs P1870 *No. 85* and P2029 *No. 87*. About this time the work I was doing at Leeds, part of which was to develop into the colliery to power stations 'Merry-go-Round' operations, was moved to an office in Derby and this resulted in weekend commuting from Derby to my home in Sussex and a cessation of photographic opportunities of British Railways and Industrial steam locomotives.

P1870, S&L Minerals, Wellingborough, *No. 87.* 1 October 1966.

Chapter Five

1967 – A Final Industrial Visit

Early in 1967 I was to take up a position at BRB Headquarters, Marylebone, which restricted all my railway photographic opportunities.

The only visit I was to make was on 10 July to Bowaters, Sittingbourne. As before all their stock was present, except of 0-4-0F *Victor*, which had been scrapped earlier in the year. I was again to photograph many of them including 0-4-2STs KS4219 *Melior* and KS926 *Leander*. The 2 foot 6 in gauge system was to close in 1969 with all of the locos going into preservation, many of them to the Sittingbourne & Kemsley Light Railway, which still uses a section of the original railway. Standard gauge steam finally finished at the end of 1970, although both locos were purchased for preservation.

I was to leave British Railways in September 1967, get married, get a mortgage and have two sons – a relatively normal life away from steam railways.

KS926, Bowaters,
Sittingbourne,
Leander. 10 July 1967.

KS4219, Bowaters, Sittingbourne, *Melior.* 10 July 1967.

The period of industrial steam photography was a short one, and perhaps I should have started earlier. However, bearing in mind I did not really start railway photography until the autumn of 1961, I think I just would not have had the time. There are many other steam locos that I saw over this period from the window of passing trains. The real regret I have was not being able to visit the quarries of North Wales. I was scheduled to go there but had to pull out at the last minute.

Chapter Six

What Happened Next?

From myself, very little. I retained my memberships of IRS and LCGB for several years but did not take part in any of their activities. However, family visits were made to some of the heritage railways – in particular the Bluebell, since it was fairly close to my home. I later started scanning my negatives and slides and started loading them onto the photographers' Flickr site. In 2010 I received a request from the Middleton Railway for use of some of my images for an event they were holding about the Manchester Ship Canal railways – a more than pleasing request, which I was happy to oblige. We went on a family visit to Middleton and I was rewarded not only by seeing large prints of my work, but also a footplate ride on 0-6-0ST MW1601 *Matthew Murray*. By coincidence the last previous footplate ride had been in 1966 at the Middleton Railway. This was on 0-6-0DE HE1697 *John Alcock* – the former LMS No. 7051. At that time the Middleton Railway was running a regular freight service that ran behind the Jack's Lane works of HE.

As can be appreciated, during the period in which I was taking industrial photographs, the numbers of steam locomotives was in decline. This decline continued at a great pace for a number of reasons; the Clean Air Act of 1968 imposed restrictions in and around populated areas, some NCB areas tried, without a large amount of success, to overcome this by fitting Hunslet Underfeed Fireboxes to some of their 'Austerity' 0-6-0STs, but the writing was on the wall. The building of large power stations, some gas-fired, some coal-fired, some nuclear-powered, meant the closure of the small local power stations. Something rather similar happened that affected gas and coke works. Possibly the major contributor was the availability of redundant British Railways diesel shunters. Changes to freight operations, 'Merry-go-Round' coal feeder services, block single-product trains, etc. led to the closure of many goods depots and marshalling yards. As a result there were large numbers of surplus Class 03, Class 08 and Class 14 locos, many of which were snapped up by industry. In fact, of the 56 Class 14s built between 1964 and 1966, no less than forty-nine went into Industrial service between 1968 and 1970. The Nationalisation of the Iron and Steel Industries led to the closure of many of the works, a decline that continues to this day. Finally, the closure of exhausted and non-cost effective collieries was capped by mass closures following the national coal miners' strike. Nowadays the only places to see steam workings, by industrial and ex-mainline locomotives, are at the various heritage railways.

Sources and Dedication

This book is dedicated to the late Malcolm Burton, who introduced me to industrial railways and was the prime organiser of so many of the trips I went on, and to Eric Tonks, whose seminal work on the ironstone railways of the Midlands inspired so many enthusiasts, and also his untiring work for both ILS and IRS.

All photographs were taken by myself, those for 1955 with a Purma Plus camera, the remainder with either a Montana TLR or a Reflexa SLR.

Reference has been made to the following publications:

Various Industrial Locomotive Handbooks published by the Industrial Railway Society and The Industrial Locomotive Society

Davies, Alan, *Locomotives of the Lancashire Central Coalfield – the Walkden Connection* (Amberley Publishing, 2014)

Davies, Alan, *Walkden Yard* (Amberley Publishing, 2013)

Tonks, Eric S, *Ironstone Railways of the Midlands* (Locomotive Publishing Co., 1959)

Thorpe, Don, *The Railways of the Manchester Ship Canal* (OPC 1984)

Mountford, Colin, *The Bowes Railway* (Industrial Railway Society/Tyne & Wear Industrial Monuments Trust, 1976)

Wear, Russell and Lees, Eric C, *Stephen Lewin and the Poole Factory* (IRS and ILS 1978)

Redman, Noel Nelson, *The Railway Foundry, Leeds 1839–1969* (Goose & Sons 1972)

Thanks have to go to all the workers at the various locations visited, in particular the then Managers at Colvilles, Mossend and RTB Elba Steelworks, all of whom are no longer on this mortal coil.

Special thanks yet again to Brian Read, who undertook the task of checking the original draft document.

Thanks also go to the good people at Amberley Publishing for their continued encouragement.

Extra special thanks have to go to my long suffering wife Gillian, who let me have use of our dining room table for the duration of the preparation and writing of this book; also to my Youngest son, Jeremy, who undertook the task of checking the printer's proof for grammatical and spelling errors.

Finally thanks to you, the reader, for getting this far.